# Fields

A Children's Story by Vernice Walker Author of A Reluctant Rodeo Queen.

We were tired of working on our farm, especially before getting to play or have fun. We didn't like going to bed early and waking up with the chickens, either. So, my siblings and I decided to let our parents know how we felt. They listened to us go on and on about how hard, hot, and sweaty it was working with Gramps in the garden, and with Daddy and his rodeo.

We shared with them that we didn't have enough time to play with our cousins and friends, ride horses, play basketball, and do all the things we thought all kids our age got to do, either.

Our parents replied to our complaints by telling us how good
they thought we had it. They shared stories about how they had
to either walk or catch a horse and ride it to get to school while
we got to ride in nice, clean buses. They went on to say that
they worked from sunup to sundown in the fields. They didn't
get to play with cousins or friends like we did. We kids were like,
Whatever.

Our Gramps and Grandma listened in, occasionally chiming in
and acknowledging that what our parents said was true.
We got a lot off our chests that weekend, and we kids thought
that from then on, things would be different.

We thought that our parents got the message and that
the days of going to bed early and waking up at the crack of
dawn would be over, too.

Towards the end of the conversation with our parents, Gramps said, "June, y'all should take the kids to the fields and let them see what it's like." Our Momma interrupted, "Oh no, I don't think they could take it in the fields." We looked at them, and I said, "If y'all could do it we can too." Gramps shook his head and said, "No, on second thought, we can't take y'all there." Our Momma looked at us and thought for a moment longer. "So y'all think we had it easy as kids, huh?" she asked. My older siblings chimed in, and my older brother said dismissively, "We can do whatever y'all did as kids – if not more."

"Would y'all like to have an experience for one day like we had every day, growing up?" our Dad asked.

We had no idea what kind of fields they were talking about, but it was settled, we were going to these fields, and we would do whatever our parents claimed they did as kids, Just as well as they did – if not better.

"It couldn't be any harder than working stooped over picking weeds out of Gramp's garden in the hot summer sun while the scary scarecrow looked on," I thought.

Gramps gave us a supply list of the things we needed for our fieldwork: heavy-duty gloves, long-sleeved shirts, long pants, old but comfortable shoes, and, lastly, a hat. "What kind of fields are these that require such shabby clothes to enter?" I thought to myself. The next weekend, our Daddy and Momma made sure we had all the required clothing – but most importantly, gloves. Gramps emphasized that we needed good and sturdy gloves, for some reason.

Momma packed us a lunch for the day: cold bologna sandwiches, chips, and cold pop. She said she and Daddy would come along later in the day to check up on us, but we'd ride with Gramps to the fields. I thought, "great!" I loved riding in the back of Gramps' truck. It was a five-speed, pea-green 1953 pickup truck. My older sister, my next-to-oldest and younger brothers, and I went along on this trip, making four of us kids in total.

Our parents woke us up early on the day of the trip, way earlier than when we usually got up. They told us that it was best to get to the fields before the sun came up.

My siblings and I put on our shabby uniforms for the field work and ate breakfast while we waited for Gramps.

11

It felt odd to wear long-sleeved shirts and long-legged pants in the middle of summer. Not long after we finished the last bite of our breakfast, we could hear Gramps out in front of our house, blowing the horn. We hurried out so we would not be late. We made our way to the back of Gramps' pickup, our usual riding spot.

I loved riding in the back bed of Gramps' pickup truck; it was the best place to sit. "We'll see y'all soon," Momma said as she waved, and we were off. Gramps drove his usual speed – fast. He'd stick his head out of his window and say, "Y'all make sure you sit down back there!" We did as he said.

He drove in a direction that I was unfamiliar with. "Are we almost there?" we kids continually asked. "Not yet," Gramps would answer patiently.

After what seemed like a much longer ride than I'd ever had in the back of Gramps' truck, he said, "We're almost there." He pointed out his window, "See those fields out yonder?" he asked us four. "What's that white stuff?" I said under my breath. Getting curious, I yelled loud enough so he could hear me as he drove over the gravelly country road. "Gramps, what's that white stuff out there?!" I asked. "It's cotton!" he replied.

By the time we'd arrived at the cotton fields, my siblings and I were sleepy and could have used a nap after the long ride.

But we didn't say anything; we were in full observation mode.
There were people already there, and some of them were kids, too.
    I thought to myself, "Maybe they spent the night here?" I couldn't
imagine anyone leaving earlier than we did that morning.

    Gramps parked his truck, and he took out a cooler of water for us
all to drink from. "Well, we're here," he said, "the Cotton Fields."
My siblings and I looked at each other. These weren't the kind of
fields we had in mind – we considered blackberry fields maybe, but
never cotton. I thought cotton fields only existed in the South. "Let's
go check in", Gramps said.

My two brothers, my sister, and I followed his lead. "We need to check in to get our sacks," he said to the man at the counter. "Our sacks? I thought. "What kind of sack could this be?" Gramps said, "Make sure to put your gloves on before getting your Croker Sacks, because they can be a bit rough." I replied, "Croker Sacks? I thought they were only used for Croker Sack races!" "Gramps had been here before," I thought. He knew the lay of the land.

He picked two of the longest Croker
Sacks they had - I'd never seen any that
long! "I'll take one like he has," I said to
the attendant. The attendant began to
laugh. Mind you, I was 10 years old,
weighing in at just 70lbs soaking wet!
He said, "I think a junior sack is what you
need." I took it reluctantly, thinking
I could fill the larger one.

20

26

Gramps, seemingly annoyed, demonstrated the pulling technique to me again. He had to show us several times before I finally got the hang of it. While pulling and putting the cotton into the Croker Sack tied at my waist, I was looking around for our Gramps.

I looked and looked for him. When I finally saw him in the distance, he was pulling two rows simultaneously! I watched in amazement. How he was able to keep two Croker Sacks – that had to be over 6' in length – tied across his shoulders and fill them at the same time, I will never know. I was just thankful my three siblings were there to witness it, because they would never have believed me otherwise. He had reached a distance where we could barely see him. "Boy, he is moving fast," I thought. "Gramps!" I yelled. "When are we taking a break?!" I asked. This wasn't quite the experience I'd envisioned.

28

My gloves kept falling off, and the sharp barbs surrounding
the cotton were sticking to me. They felt like needles. I was trying
my best, but I was pulling the entire plant from the ground, which was
an absolute no-no. Finally, I sat down in the sandy, tan-colored dirt,
frustrated and exhausted. I'd had it with this assignment! I was tired,
and it was beginning to get hot in the long-sleeved getup, too.

The weigh station wasn't far from the check-in location. I was ready to check my Croker Sack in and see how much I'd earned from this monotonous cotton picking, pulling, or whatever you want to call it, assignment. I tried pulling my bag to the weigh station, but it was too heavy! My sister and I pulled it as far as we could, but my older brother had to help us get it the rest of the way there. "75 cents!" the man at the weight machine said, loudly and without hesitation, and promptly handed me three quarters.

I looked at the man, accepted the three coins, and went to
Gramps' truck for a cold drink. I was done with this experiment of
an experience and was ready to go home. I wondered,
"Where are our parents?" My siblings weighed in and cashed out;
they didn't fare much better than I did, either.

They joined me at the back of Gramps' truck, where we ate
the cold bologna sandwiches, chips, and soda our
Mom had packed. I'm not sure how much my Gramps made
that day, but he earned every penny and then some,
as far as I was concerned.

35

Our parents showed up not long after Gramps cashed out. "Well, what do y'all think?" our Mom asked. "Would you guys prefer to work in the fields every day instead of helping your Gramps and me occasionally on the weekends?" our Dad asked. We had no comment, nor do I recall complaining quite as much about the hard work in our Gramps' garden or Daddy's Rodeo after our field experience.

This true story is dedicated to
the loving memory of:

John Walker AKA Gramps
May 21, 1907 – April 27, 1983